WILD WICKED WONDERFUL

TOP 10:

DEFENDERS

By Virginia Loh-Hagan

45th Parallel Press

Published in the United States of America by Cherry Lake Publishing
Ann Arbor, Michigan
www.cherrylakepublishing.com

Content Adviser: Stephen Ditchkoff, Professor of Wildlife Ecology and Management, Auburn University, Alabama
Reading Adviser: Marla Conn MS, Ed., Literacy specialist, Read-Ability, Inc.

Book Designer: Melinda Millward

Photo Credits: ©vanchai/Shutterstock.com, cover, 1, 21; ©Digital Vision/Thinkstock, 5; ©Fabio Maffei/Shutterstock.com, 6; ©belizar/Shutterstock.com, 6; ©Steve Bower/Shutterstock.com, 6; ©Leah Smalley/Dreamstime.com, 7; ©Svetlana Foote/Shutterstock.com, 8; ©Auscape/Getty Images, 10; ©Lazydaz/Dreamstime.com, 10; ©Darlyne A Murawski/Getty Images, 11; ©Ryan M. Bolton/Shutterstock.com, 12; ©Marc Parsons/Dreamstime.com, 12; ©danz13/Shutterstock.com, 12; ©Martha Marks/Shutterstock.com, 13; ©Decent-Exposure-Photography/iStockphoto, 14; ©Arto Hakola/Shutterstock.com, 14; ©Asmus Koefoed/Shutterstock.com, 14; ©imageBROKER/Alamy Stock Photo, 15; ©CuttsNaturePhotography/Thinkstock, 16; ©Joe McDonald/Shutterstock.com, 16; ©Ingram Publishing/Thinkstock, 16; ©Rinus Baak/Dreamstime.com, 17; ©Matt Jeppson/Shutterstock.com, 18; ©EMPPhotography/iStockphoto, 20; ©tratong/Shutterstock.com, 20; ©Brian Kinney/Shutterstock.com, 20; ©davemhuntphotography/Shutterstock.com, 22; ©Audrey Snider-Bell/Shutterstock.com, 22; ©Andrea Mangoni/Shutterstock.com, 23; ©saasemen/Shutterstock.com, 24; ©Four Oaks/Shutterstock.com, 24; ©Dreidos/Shutterstock.com, 24; ©Bildagentur Zoonar GmbH/Shutterstock.com, 25; ©ANZAV/Thinkstock, 26; ©Natursports/Shutterstock.com, 27; ©smuay/Thinkstock, 28; ©Orionmystery/Dreamstime.com, 29; ©Guillermo Nunez Mira/Dreamstime.com, 30; ©Zsschreiner/Shutterstock.com, 30; ©Hue Chee Kong/Shutterstock.com, 30; ©Andrey Davidenko/Dreamstime.com, 31

Graphic Element Credits: ©tukkki/Shutterstock.com, back cover, front cover, multiple interior pages; ©paprika/Shutterstock.com, back cover, front cover, multiple interior pages; ©Silhouette Lover/Shutterstock Images, multiple interior pages

45th Parallel Press is an imprint of Cherry Lake Publishing.

Library of Congress Cataloging-in-Publication Data

Names: Loh-Hagan, Virginia.
Title: Top 10—defenders / by Virginia Loh-Hagan.
Description: Ann Arbor : Cherry Lake Publishing, 2016. | Series: Wild wicked wonderful |
    Includes bibliographical references and index.
Identifiers: LCCN 2015050701| ISBN 9781634711005 (hardcover) | ISBN 9781634711999 (pdf) |
    ISBN 9781634712989 (pbk.) | ISBN 9781634713979 (ebook)
Subjects: LCSH: Animal defenses—Juvenile literature.
Classification: LCC QL759 .L64 2016 | DDC 591.47—dc23
LC record available at https://lccn.loc.gov/2015050701

Printed in the United States of America
Corporate Graphics

About the Author

Dr. Virginia Loh-Hagan is an author, university professor, former classroom teacher, and curriculum designer. Her greatest defense weapon is her big mouth. She lives in San Diego with her very tall husband and very naughty dogs. To learn more about her, visit www.virginialoh.com.

TABLE OF CONTENTS

INTRODUCTION

Animals live in an unsafe world. They **defend** themselves. They fight against nature. Weather conditions can be harsh. Their environments can be harsh. They fight against **predators**. Predators are hunters. They hunt for **prey**. Prey are animals hunted for food.

Animals must stop attacks. They protect themselves. They protect their families. They don't want to be in danger. They don't want to be eaten.

Some animals defend themselves in extreme ways. Their defenses are bigger. Their defenses are better. They have the most exciting defenses in the animal world!

Some animals defend themselves against humans.

5

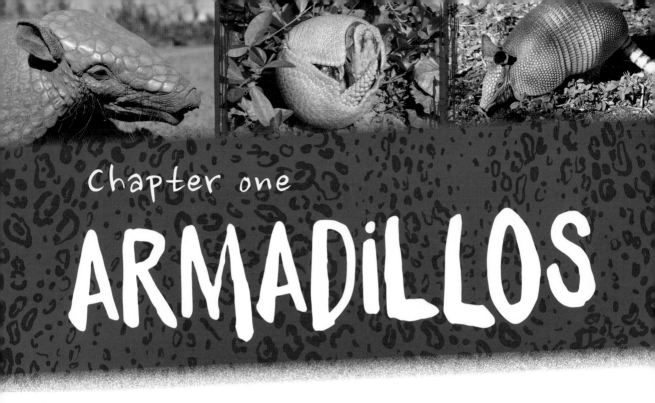

Chapter one

ARMADILLOS

Armadillos are from South America. They can also be found in the southern United States. *Armadillo* is a Spanish word. It means "man in **armor**." Armadillos' shells are like armor. Armor is tough, bony plates. They protect soft muscles and tissues.

Armadillos' shells cover the top of their bodies. Top shells are called **carapaces**. They're strong. Dogs' sharp teeth can't cut their shells. These shells are their main defense. When in danger, they hide in their shells. They wait. Most predators get bored.

Armadillos' undersides have soft skin and fur.

Most armadillos cannot roll into a ball. They have too many plates. But three-banded armadillos can. They fold their bodies. They hide all their body parts.

Armadillos' greatest danger is cars. Moving cars crush their shells.

Armadillos don't have strong bites. They can't fight. So, they depend on their shells. But they have other defenses.

They stay still. They hope predators ignore them. If not, they run and hide. They have short legs. But they move quickly. They run into thorny bushes. Their shells protect them from thorns. But predators aren't protected. Thorns hurt them.

Armadillos have sharp claws. They're diggers. They dig for food. They dig dens. They dig to hide from predators. They wedge themselves in holes. They spread out their shells. This makes them hard to pick up.

DID YOU KNOW...?

- People have thumbs. Our thumbs stand upright. Thumbs help us use tools and weapons. This is how we defend ourselves.

- Termites fart more than other animals.

- Tardigrades are the first animals to survive in outer space.

- Armadillo shells have been used to make guitar-like instruments.

- Porcupine quills are dirty. They cause infection. If they break, they're difficult to pull out.

- Burglars tend not to steal from houses with dogs. Top dog guard breeds include German shepherds, Dobermans, and Rottweilers.

- Bees see all colors except for red.

chapter two

MOTH BUTTERFLY CATERPILLARS

Moth butterfly caterpillars live in forests. They live in treetops. They live in Asia and Australia. They live inside green tree ant nests. These ants are dangerous. They have powerful jaws. They spit jets of poison. But they don't hurt moth butterfly caterpillars.

These caterpillars have carapaces. They don't feel ant bites. Their shells protect them. They're tough. They're like leather. They're too heavy for ants to flip over.

Moth butterfly caterpillars use green tree ants for protection and food.

The caterpillars eat ant babies. They become moth butterflies. They lose their shells. They're open for attacks. But their wings have slippery scales. They fly away unharmed.

Chapter three
TURTLES

Turtles live everywhere except Antarctica. They have powerful shells. Their tops and bottoms are covered. They're built like tanks. Their shells are made of over 60 **fused** bones. Fused means joined together. Their shells are attached to their ribs and spine. Turtles can't crawl out of their shells.

Most turtles can hide in their shells. They stay still. They trick predators. They look like rocks. Some turtle shells can support a lot of weight. They're hard to break. Most predators give up.

Turtles have carapaces and plastrons. Plastrons are shells that cover the undersides.

Alligator snapping turtles have sharp claws. They have powerful jaws. Their jaws can snap through bone.

chapter four

TOMATO FROGS

Tomato frogs live in Madagascar. They're bright red. Their color is one defense. The color warns predators to stay away. But some snakes don't care. They like eating frogs.

Tomato frogs make themselves hard to swallow. First, they puff up their bodies. They try to look big and scary. Next, they release a thick, white glue. They only do this when scared. This glue gums up the snakes' eyes and mouths. Snakes release the frogs. The glue is hard to get rid of.

Some humans react badly to this glue. They get rashes. They get sick.

Tomato frogs look like fat, round tomatoes.

chapter five

HORNED LIZARDS

Horned lizards live in North and Central America. They have a crown of horns. They have many spines on their backs. They're small. They have many predators. They need different defenses.

They puff up their bodies. They look twice their size. They look like spiky balloons. They make themselves hard to swallow.

They have special coloring. They can be yellow. They can be gray. They can be red. They can be brown. They **camouflage**. They stay still. They blend into their

Horned lizards use camouflage to prey on ants and other insects.

environments. They hide. They're hard to find.

They sprint. They stop. They try to look blurry. They confuse predators.

Horned lizards move their body around to avoid the jaws of predators.

Some horned lizards have a special defense. Their eyes shoot blood. They have **ducts** in the corners of their eyes. Ducts are like tubes. They stop the blood flowing in their heads. They swell up. They increase the blood pressure. Then, the ducts burst.

The blood can shoot 5 feet (1.5 meters). It blinds predators. Predators get confused. They get distracted. Horned lizards have time to run away.

There's something in the blood. It tastes gross to dogs, wolves, and coyotes. Horned lizards don't squirt at humans. Humans don't scare them enough.

Humans Do What?!?

Eugene Tsui is an architect. He designed his parents' house. It looks like a water bug. He created one of the world's safest houses. Tsui's house can survive fires, earthquakes, flooding, and termites. Nature inspired his house design. He based the house shape on tardigrades. Tardigrades are tiny water animals. They're able to live in extreme conditions. The house has round and oval shapes with a lot of arches. He used concrete to copy the structure of the cholla cactus. This cactus is fireproof. The heating system for the house is based on the bone and vein structures of two dinosaurs. The surface is based on fish scales. Tsui said this house "is designed as nature would design for safety."

Chapter six

PORCUPINES

Porcupines live in North America, South America, and Africa. They have sharp **quills**. Quills are sharp spines, or needles. Quills are on their backs, sides, and tails. New quills replace old ones. Quills lay flat. They stand up when porcupines are in danger. They cause great pain. They cut into organs. They cause death.

Porcupines don't hide. They make loud noises. They stamp their feet. They rattle their quills. They move backward. They ram their quills into predators' faces.

Porcupine quills can be 1 foot (30.5 centimeters) long.

Quill tips have hundreds of tiny **barbs**. Barbs are sharp. They're prickly. They get stuck in skin. Skin swells. The barbs are hard to pull out.

Chapter seven

TARANTULAS

Tarantulas live in the southern part of the world. Some have special hair. They have stinging hair. Hairs cover their bodies. The hairs have barbs. They're like tiny fishhooks. Tarantulas can fire their hairs. They aim and shoot. Their hairs are like darts.

Tarantulas get ready. They strike. They stand on their first two legs. They stretch out their back legs. They stretch toward predators. They rub their legs against their stomachs. They flick their hairs. They aim for eyes. They aim up noses.

Some tarantulas bite instead of flicking their hairs.

Their hairs blind. They cause rashes. They cause pain.

Chapter eight

DOgs

Dogs came from wolves. Wolves are fierce. They're wild. They're predators. They live in **packs**. A pack is a group of wolves. Their leader is the **alpha** male. Alpha means the boss. Alphas are the strongest wolves. They get the best food. They get the best sleeping spots. They defend their wolf packs.

Wolves and humans were enemies. Then, humans tamed wolves. Wolves changed to dogs. Dogs became our pets. Dogs see humans as their alphas. Humans are their owners. Humans are their masters.

Wolves are intelligent, social animals.

Dogs live with humans all over the world. Dogs defend their humans. They defend their **territories**. Territories are areas.

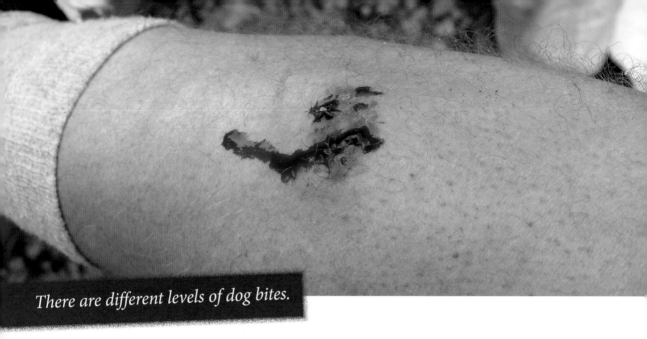

There are different levels of dog bites.

Dogs are great guards. They share many wolf behaviors. They show their teeth. They growl. They bite.

Dog bites draw blood. They can be deadly. They're more dangerous than bites from bears, alligators, and spiders combined! Dog spit has germs. Victims could get **rabies**. Rabies is a bad sickness. It kills over 55,000 people a year.

Dogs are fast. They have good aim. They have strong jaws. They have sharp teeth. They don't let go. They tear muscles and skin. They bite through chests. They damage organs. They're great defenders.

WHEN ANIMALS ATTACK!

Bullfighters have an odd and dangerous job. They get in a big arena. They make a bull angry. They encourage the bull to attack. They make bulls run at them. Then, they try to escape the bulls. They try to kill the bulls. But some don't escape. Bulls defend themselves by attacking. They're powerful beasts. They're strong. They have sharp horns. Many bullfighters have gotten injured. Many have died. Lorenzo Sanchez was about to kill a bull. The bull threw him in the air. The bull's horn gored his left leg. Sanchez hit the ground. The bull gored his chest. But more bulls have died than bullfighters. Many people don't like this sport.

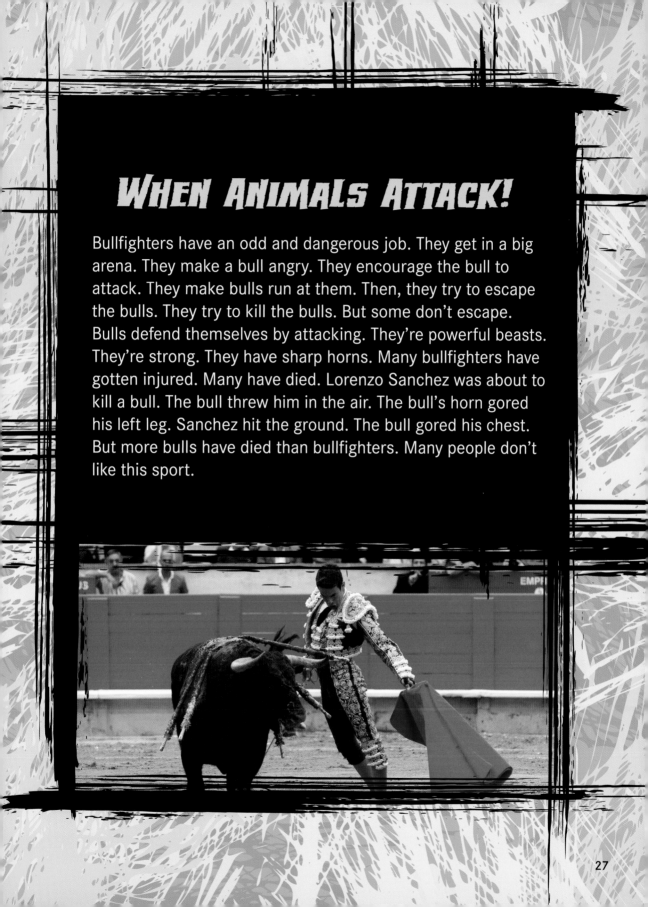

Chapter nine

TERMiTES

Termites live around the world. Most live in tropical areas. They're found in dark, damp places. They eat wood. They live as a **colony**. A colony is a group. They work together.

Colonies have soldier termites. They defend the colony. Every 100 termites has 20 soldiers. Soldier termites have sharp jaws. They have nozzles on their foreheads. They spray sticky glue. The glue traps victims. It makes victims unable to move.

The United States has about 50 species of termites.

Some termites don't live in colonies. They don't have soldiers. These termites have special stomachs. Their guts explode when attacked. The gut juices are dangerous.

Chapter ten

BEES

Bees live almost everywhere. They can't live in extreme cold. They live in colonies. They defend their queen bees. They defend their nests.

Worker bees have stingers. The stingers have **venom**. Venom is injected poison. When one bee stings, it sends a message. Other bees come. They're ready to sting. They're prepared to die.

Bees attack as **swarms**. A swarm is a bunch of angry bees. Swarms are deadly. They can take down predators. The bees attack together.

Honey bees die after they sting. The stinger pulls out their stomachs.

Africanized honeybees are deadly. They attack 20 times faster. They sting eight times more. They chase predators up to 1 mile (1.6 kilometers). They sting over and over again.

CONSIDER THIS!

TAKE A POSITION! Animals in zoos are protected. Zookeepers work hard to keep animals safe. But these animals do not know how to defend themselves. They cannot be released into the wild. What do you think about this? Are zoos helping or harming animals? Argue your point with reasons and evidence.

SAY WHAT? Read *Extreme Predators*. This is another 45th Parallel Press book by Virginia Loh-Hagan. Compare the predators to the defenders in this book. Explain how they are similar. Explain how they are different.

THINK ABOUT IT! All animals have to eat. So, animals can be both predators and prey. Sometimes, they have to attack to eat. Sometimes they have to defend themselves. Create a food chain using animals featured in this series.

LEARN MORE!

- Johnson, Rebecca L. *When Lunch Fights Back: Wickedly Clever Animal Defenses*. Minneapolis: Millbrook Press, 2015.
- Rake, Jody Sullivan. *Spines, Horns, and Armor: Animal Weapons and Defenses*. Mankato, MN: Capstone Press, 2012.

GLOSSARY

alpha (AL-fuh) the animal in charge of a group

armor (AHR-mur) hard, tough, bony plates; protective cover

barbs (BAHRBZ) sharp and prickly points

camouflage (KAM-uh-flahzh) hide by blending into the environment

carapaces (KER-uh-pace-iz) protective top shell

colony (KAH-luh-nee) a large group of animals that live together

defend (dih-FEND) protect, guard

ducts (DUHKTS) tubes that carry liquid or air from one place to another

fused (FYOOZD) joined together

packs (PAKS) groups of wolves

predators (PRED-uh-turz) hunters

prey (PRAY) animals that are hunted for food

quills (KWILZ) sharp spines or needles

rabies (RAY-beez) a bad sickness spread by some animals

swarms (SWORMZ) angry mobs

territories (TER-ih-tor-eez) defended areas

venom (VEN-uhm) poison injected under the skin

INDEX